Table of Contents

Chapter 1: SUI Unveiled: The Ultimate Guide to the SUI Ecosystem........1
Introduction to SUI..1
Key Features of the SUI Ecosystem...3
SUI's Position in the Blockchain Landscape.............................6
Benefits of Engaging with the SUI Ecosystem 8

Chapter 2: SUI Blockchain Technology Overview....................................11
Architecture of the SUI Blockchain..11
Consensus Mechanisms Used in SUI 13
Scalability Solutions in SUI 16
Comparison with Other Blockchain Technologies..................18

Chapter 3: SUI Smart Contracts and Development 22
Introduction to Smart Contracts on SUI 22
Development Tools and Frameworks.......................................24
Writing and Deploying Smart Contracts 27
Best Practices for Smart Contract Development....................29

Chapter 4: SUI Decentralized Applications (dApps) 33
Overview of dApps on the SUI Blockchain.............................33
Popular dApps in the SUI Ecosystem......................................35
Developing dApps on SUI..38
User Experience and Interface Design Considerations...........40

Chapter 5: SUI Governance and Community Involvement 43
Understanding SUI Governance Models..................................43
Role of the Community in Decision-Making...........................45
Participating in Governance Proposals....................................48
Building and Sustaining Community Engagement 50

Chapter 6: SUI Security Protocols and Best Practices...........................54
Overview of Security in Blockchain 54
Security Features of the SUI Blockchain 56
Common Vulnerabilities and Threats......................................59
Best Practices for Ensuring Security 61

Chapter 7: SUI Use Cases in Various Industries......................................65
Financial Services and Banking..65
Supply Chain Management...67
Healthcare Applications 70
Gaming and Entertainment 72

Chapter 8: SUI Roadmap and Future Developments............................76
Current Status of the SUI Blockchain.....................................76
Upcoming Features and Enhancements..................................78
Long-Term Vision for SUI 81
Challenges and Opportunities Ahead.......................................83

Chapter 1: SUI Unveiled: The Ultimate Guide to the SUI Ecosystem

Introduction to SUI

SUI represents a cutting-edge development in the blockchain landscape, introducing a new paradigm that promises to enhance the way digital assets and applications are managed. At its core, SUI is designed to offer a scalable, secure, and user-friendly platform that caters to a diverse array of users, from cryptocurrency enthusiasts to retail investors. The architecture of SUI is built to support high transaction throughput while maintaining low latency, addressing some of the critical challenges faced by existing blockchain technologies. This introduction sets the stage for understanding the significance of SUI in the broader ecosystem of decentralized finance and beyond.

One of the standout features of SUI is its innovative approach to smart contracts. Unlike traditional models that often struggle with performance and complexity, SUI's smart contract framework is designed to be both powerful and accessible. This opens up new avenues for developers, enabling them to create decentralized applications (dApps) that can operate efficiently and reliably. As we delve deeper into the details of SUI's smart contracts in future sections, you will discover how this technology empowers developers and enhances user experiences in the growing world of decentralized applications.

SUI is not just about technological advancements; it also emphasizes community involvement and governance. The SUI ecosystem operates on principles of decentralization, encouraging users to participate actively in decision-making processes that shape the platform's future. This aspect of SUI plays a crucial role in fostering a sense of ownership among its users, promoting a vibrant community that contributes to the platform's growth and sustainability. The forthcoming discussions on governance mechanisms will shed light on how stakeholders can influence the evolution of SUI.

Security is paramount in the world of cryptocurrencies, and SUI prioritizes robust security protocols to protect its users and their assets. By implementing advanced security measures, SUI aims to create a trustworthy environment for transactions and interactions within its ecosystem. This focus on security is critical in a landscape where vulnerabilities can lead to significant losses. As we explore SUI's security protocols and best practices, you will learn how the platform mitigates risks and safeguards user assets against potential threats.

Finally, the versatility of SUI extends to its use cases across various industries. From finance and supply chain management to gaming and social networking, SUI's blockchain technology is poised to revolutionize how businesses operate. The potential applications are vast, and the roadmap for SUI's future developments indicates a commitment to continuous innovation and adaptation. In the subsequent chapters, we will explore specific use cases and the strategic direction of SUI, providing you with insights into how this technology can impact various sectors and contribute to the evolution of the digital economy.

Key Features of the SUI Ecosystem

The SUI ecosystem is characterized by a set of innovative features that position it as a leading player in the cryptocurrency landscape. Central to its architecture is the SUI blockchain, which is designed to provide high throughput and low latency, making it suitable for a wide range of applications. This high-performance capability is complemented by a unique consensus mechanism that ensures transactions are processed swiftly and efficiently. As a result, developers and users alike can expect a seamless experience when engaging with the ecosystem, whether they are participating in decentralized finance (DeFi) or exploring non-fungible tokens (NFTs).

Smart contracts are another cornerstone of the SUI ecosystem, enabling developers to create complex decentralized applications (dApps) with ease. These contracts are built using a specialized programming language that prioritizes safety and efficiency, allowing for the creation of robust applications that can handle various use cases. By providing comprehensive documentation and development tools, SUI encourages innovation and fosters a vibrant community of developers who contribute to the ecosystem's growth. This emphasis on user-friendly development lowers the barrier to entry for aspiring creators in the blockchain space.

Governance within the SUI ecosystem is designed to be community-driven, empowering users to play an active role in decision-making processes. Token holders are granted voting rights, allowing them to influence key developments and changes within the network. This democratic approach not only enhances transparency but also ensures that the ecosystem evolves in a manner that reflects the interests of its participants. The active involvement of the community helps cultivate a sense of ownership, further strengthening the network's resilience and adaptability.

Security protocols are paramount within the SUI ecosystem, as the project prioritizes the protection of user assets and data. The platform employs advanced cryptographic techniques and decentralized security measures to safeguard against potential threats. Regular audits and a commitment to best practices in security enhance user confidence, making SUI an attractive option for retail investors and casual users alike. Furthermore, educational resources are made available to help users understand how to navigate the ecosystem safely, ensuring they can engage with peace of mind.

As the SUI ecosystem continues to evolve, its roadmap outlines ambitious plans for future developments. This includes the introduction of new features, partnerships with industry leaders, and expansion into various sectors, such as gaming and supply chain management. By actively seeking to integrate with diverse industries, SUI aims to broaden its use cases and enhance its utility. The forward-thinking approach of the ecosystem not only captures the interest of cryptocurrency enthusiasts but also positions SUI as a formidable contender in the rapidly changing landscape of digital assets.

SUI's Position in the Blockchain Landscape

SUI has emerged as a significant player in the rapidly evolving blockchain landscape, distinguished by its unique architecture and innovative features. Designed to enhance scalability and efficiency, SUI utilizes a novel approach that allows for parallel transaction execution. This capability addresses one of the critical limitations faced by many existing blockchain networks, particularly in handling large volumes of transactions simultaneously. As a result, SUI appeals to a broad audience, including retail investors and cryptocurrency enthusiasts, who seek a platform that can facilitate faster and more reliable transactions.

The architecture of SUI is rooted in a move towards a more user-friendly and accessible blockchain experience. By prioritizing simplicity and developer experience, SUI enables the creation of decentralized applications (dApps) with ease. This focus on usability is particularly attractive to new developers and those exploring the blockchain for the first time. With SUI's smart contract capabilities, developers can engage with the ecosystem to build a diverse range of applications, from financial services to gaming, thus expanding its reach and functionality in multiple industries.

Governance and community involvement are integral to SUI's position in the blockchain landscape. By fostering a robust community, SUI ensures that its development is guided by user needs and preferences. This collaborative approach not only strengthens the network but also encourages active participation from stakeholders. Retail investors and meme coin enthusiasts alike can engage in governance processes, shaping the future of the SUI ecosystem. This democratic framework aids in building trust and transparency, essential elements in the cryptocurrency space.

Security remains a paramount concern in any blockchain network, and SUI has implemented rigorous protocols to protect its users and their assets. By employing best practices in security, such as regular audits and comprehensive testing, SUI aims to mitigate risks associated with smart contracts and dApps. This commitment to security not only enhances user confidence but also positions SUI as a trustworthy option for those looking to invest or develop within the ecosystem.

Looking ahead, SUI's roadmap is filled with promising developments that are set to further solidify its position within the blockchain landscape. With ongoing enhancements in technology and a commitment to community engagement, SUI is poised for significant growth. As it continues to attract interest from various sectors, the potential for innovative use cases expands, paving the way for new opportunities in the ever-changing world of cryptocurrencies. The future of SUI not only reflects its technological advancements but also its dedication to fostering a vibrant and inclusive community.

Benefits of Engaging with the SUI Ecosystem

Engaging with the SUI ecosystem offers a multitude of benefits for individuals interested in cryptocurrencies, retail investors, and meme coin enthusiasts. One of the most significant advantages is the opportunity to participate in a rapidly evolving blockchain technology that emphasizes scalability and efficiency. The SUI blockchain is designed to handle a high throughput of transactions, making it an attractive option for those looking to invest in a platform that can support a wide array of decentralized applications (dApps). This high performance ensures that users can enjoy seamless interactions without the delays often associated with other blockchain networks, enhancing overall user experience.

Another key benefit of engaging with the SUI ecosystem is the potential for innovation through smart contracts. SUI's smart contract functionality allows developers to create complex, automated agreements that can facilitate various transactions without the need for intermediaries. This not only reduces costs but also increases transparency and security. For retail investors and those interested in meme coins, this opens up new avenues for creating unique projects that can attract community interest and investment. The ease of developing and deploying smart contracts on SUI encourages creativity and the potential for groundbreaking applications.

Community involvement is a cornerstone of the SUI ecosystem. The platform promotes active participation in governance, allowing users to influence decisions that affect the ecosystem's development. This democratic approach fosters a sense of ownership among participants, making them more invested in the success of the SUI network. For individuals who enjoy being part of a community-driven initiative, engaging with SUI can provide a fulfilling experience. Moreover, the collaborative nature of the ecosystem encourages knowledge sharing and networking, which can lead to new opportunities and partnerships.

Security is paramount in the world of cryptocurrencies, and the SUI ecosystem prioritizes robust security protocols to protect its users. Engaging with SUI means benefiting from advanced security measures that help safeguard investments and personal data. This focus on security is particularly appealing to retail investors who may be cautious about entering the volatile cryptocurrency market. By choosing a platform with strong security practices, participants can engage with confidence, knowing that their assets are well-protected against potential threats.

Lastly, the future developments within the SUI ecosystem present exciting opportunities for growth and expansion. The roadmap laid out for SUI includes plans for continuous upgrades and new features that aim to enhance the platform's usability and functionality. For those interested in the long-term potential of blockchain technology, keeping an eye on SUI's progress can be advantageous. As more industries begin to adopt SUI's innovative solutions, early engagement can lead to significant rewards for those who recognize the potential of this emerging ecosystem.

Chapter 2: SUI Blockchain Technology Overview

Architecture of the SUI Blockchain

The architecture of the SUI blockchain is designed to offer scalability, security, and flexibility, making it an appealing choice for a wide range of applications within the cryptocurrency ecosystem. At its core, SUI employs a unique consensus mechanism that integrates aspects of both proof of stake and proof of history, promoting efficient transaction validation while minimizing energy consumption. This hybrid approach not only enhances the network's throughput but also ensures a level of decentralization that is crucial for maintaining trust among users. By leveraging this architecture, SUI can accommodate a growing number of transactions without sacrificing performance, which is essential for the increasing demands of decentralized applications and smart contracts.

One of the standout features of the SUI blockchain architecture is its modular design. This allows developers to create and deploy custom functionalities tailored to specific use cases, facilitating the development of decentralized applications (dApps). The modularity extends to the network's storage and execution layers, enabling developers to optimize resources and improve efficiency. As a result, applications built on SUI can achieve faster response times and reduced latency, enhancing user experience and encouraging broader adoption among retail investors and cryptocurrency enthusiasts alike.

Smart contracts on the SUI blockchain are also crafted with a focus on security and simplicity. The architecture incorporates advanced programming languages that prioritize safety, allowing developers to write contracts that are less prone to vulnerabilities. This emphasis on security is crucial, especially in a landscape where exploits and hacks can jeopardize user funds and overall trust in the ecosystem. By providing robust tools and frameworks, SUI empowers developers to build secure applications that inspire confidence among users, further driving engagement and investment.

Governance within the SUI ecosystem is another vital aspect of its architecture. The blockchain employs a decentralized governance model that allows stakeholders to participate in decision-making processes. This model ensures that the community has a voice in the future development of the network, fostering a sense of ownership and commitment among users. By engaging the community in governance, SUI not only enhances transparency but also cultivates a collaborative environment where users can contribute to the evolution of the blockchain, making it more responsive to the needs and preferences of its constituents.

Finally, the SUI blockchain architecture is designed with future scalability in mind. As the demand for blockchain technology continues to grow, SUI's infrastructure is built to adapt to evolving requirements. The roadmap for SUI includes plans for further enhancements in scalability, interoperability with other blockchains, and the introduction of innovative features that will keep it at the forefront of the industry. By investing in a resilient and forward-thinking architecture, SUI positions itself as a promising player in the cryptocurrency landscape, appealing to both seasoned investors and newcomers exploring the world of digital assets.

Consensus Mechanisms Used in SUI

Consensus mechanisms are at the heart of blockchain technology, ensuring that all participants within a network agree on the state of the ledger. In the context of SUI, a novel blockchain ecosystem, the consensus mechanism plays a crucial role in maintaining security, scalability, and efficiency. SUI employs a unique approach that blends elements from established consensus methods, optimizing for high throughput and low latency while ensuring decentralization and resilience against attacks.

One of the primary consensus mechanisms utilized in SUI is the Byzantine Fault Tolerance (BFT) model. This mechanism is designed to allow the network to continue functioning correctly even when some nodes fail or act maliciously. BFT is instrumental in maintaining the integrity of transactions and state changes within the SUI ecosystem. By implementing a variant of BFT, SUI can achieve consensus rapidly, making it suitable for applications that demand immediate finality, such as decentralized finance (DeFi) protocols and real-time trading platforms.

In addition to BFT, SUI incorporates a proof-of-stake (PoS) component that incentivizes token holders to participate in the validation process. This not only enhances security but also promotes a more decentralized network structure. By allowing stakeholders to stake their tokens, SUI ensures that those who have a vested interest in the network's success play a role in its governance and operation. This mechanism aligns the incentives of individual users with the broader goals of the SUI ecosystem, fostering community engagement and support.

Moreover, SUI's consensus mechanism is designed to be energy-efficient, addressing one of the significant criticisms of traditional blockchain systems. By reducing the computational workload typically associated with proof-of-work systems, SUI minimizes its environmental impact while maintaining robust security. This sustainable approach is particularly appealing to environmentally conscious investors and developers looking to build applications that align with modern sustainability goals.

As the SUI ecosystem continues to evolve, its consensus mechanisms will likely adapt to meet the demands of emerging technologies and applications. With the ongoing development of decentralized applications (dApps) and the integration of smart contracts, SUI's consensus framework will need to support increasingly complex transactions and interactions. Understanding these mechanisms is vital for anyone involved in the SUI ecosystem, from casual investors to developers looking to create next-generation blockchain solutions.

Scalability Solutions in SUI

Scalability is a critical consideration in the evolving landscape of blockchain technology, and the SUI ecosystem is no exception. As the demand for blockchain applications grows, it becomes increasingly important to develop solutions that can handle a high volume of transactions without compromising on performance or user experience. SUI has embraced this challenge by implementing innovative strategies designed to enhance its scalability, ensuring that the platform remains viable for both current and future applications.

One of the primary scalability solutions in SUI is its unique architecture, which leverages a modular design. This architecture allows for the separation of consensus and execution layers, enabling the network to process transactions more efficiently. By decoupling these functions, SUI can optimize each layer independently, resulting in faster transaction speeds and reduced latency. This design not only facilitates a smoother user experience but also allows developers to build more complex decentralized applications (dApps) that can cater to a wider range of use cases.

In addition to its architectural advantages, SUI employs advanced sharding techniques to further enhance scalability. Sharding is a method that divides the blockchain network into smaller, more manageable pieces, or shards. Each shard processes its transactions and smart contracts independently, which significantly increases the overall throughput of the network. With this approach, SUI can handle multiple transactions simultaneously, making it exceptionally well-suited for high-demand environments, such as those found in retail and gaming sectors.

To complement its architectural and sharding innovations, SUI has also integrated layer-2 solutions that facilitate off-chain transactions. These solutions allow for a greater number of transactions to be processed without congesting the main blockchain. By enabling off-chain interactions, SUI reduces the load on its network while maintaining security and transparency. This flexibility is particularly appealing to retail investors and developers, as it offers a way to scale their applications without incurring high transaction fees often associated with congested networks.

Finally, the community involvement in SUI's ongoing development plays a pivotal role in its scalability strategies. The SUI governance model encourages active participation from stakeholders, allowing them to contribute ideas and feedback on scalability initiatives. This collaborative approach not only fosters innovation but also ensures that the solutions implemented are aligned with the needs of users and developers alike. As the SUI ecosystem continues to grow, its commitment to scalability will undoubtedly enhance its appeal to a broad audience, including meme coin enthusiasts and serious investors eager to explore new opportunities in the cryptocurrency space.

Comparison with Other Blockchain Technologies

When examining SUI in the context of other blockchain technologies, it is essential to highlight its unique features and advantages. Unlike traditional blockchains like Bitcoin and Ethereum, which rely on proof-of-work and proof-of-stake mechanisms, SUI introduces a novel architecture that emphasizes scalability and low latency. This architecture allows for rapid transaction processing, making it particularly suitable for applications requiring high throughput, such as decentralized finance (DeFi) and gaming platforms. By leveraging a more efficient consensus model, SUI can handle significantly more transactions per second, positioning itself as a viable alternative for developers and users seeking faster and more efficient blockchain solutions.

Comparatively, SUI's approach to smart contracts distinguishes it from other notable platforms. While Ethereum pioneered the concept of smart contracts, SUI enhances this functionality with a more intuitive programming model. This allows developers to create complex decentralized applications (dApps) with greater ease and flexibility. SUI's smart contract environment supports multiple programming languages, catering to a broader range of developers. This adaptability fosters innovation within the SUI ecosystem, enabling the rapid development of applications across various sectors, from finance to supply chain management.

Another area where SUI stands out is its governance model. Unlike many blockchain platforms that rely on centralized entities or limited community participation, SUI promotes a more inclusive governance structure. This model empowers community members to actively participate in decision-making processes, ensuring that the platform evolves in alignment with the interests of its users. By incorporating decentralized governance mechanisms, SUI not only enhances its legitimacy but also fosters a sense of ownership among its participants, which can drive greater engagement and investment in the ecosystem.

Security is a paramount concern in the blockchain space, and SUI addresses this issue with robust protocols. While other platforms have faced significant security breaches, SUI implements advanced security measures that prioritize the integrity of transactions and user data. The use of formal verification techniques ensures that smart contracts operate as intended, minimizing vulnerabilities that could be exploited. Additionally, SUI's commitment to regular audits and community vigilance creates an environment where security is continuously prioritized, further enhancing user confidence in the platform.

In conclusion, SUI presents a compelling alternative to existing blockchain technologies through its innovative features and user-centric approach. Its scalability, flexible smart contract environment, inclusive governance model, and strong security protocols position it as a noteworthy contender in the blockchain landscape. As the cryptocurrency space continues to evolve, understanding the distinctions between SUI and other platforms will be crucial for investors and enthusiasts seeking to navigate these developments effectively. By embracing the unique advantages of SUI, stakeholders can better appreciate its potential impact on the future of decentralized applications and the broader blockchain ecosystem.

Chapter 3: SUI Smart Contracts and Development

Introduction to Smart Contracts on SUI

Smart contracts represent a transformative element in the realm of blockchain technology, and their implementation on the SUI blockchain is no exception. These self-executing contracts, where the terms are directly written into code, allow for automated, trustless transactions without the need for intermediaries. For those interested in cryptocurrencies, smart contracts on SUI provide an innovative way to facilitate agreements and transactions, making them a vital component of the SUI ecosystem. This subchapter will introduce the fundamentals of smart contracts, their significance within the SUI framework, and their potential applications for various stakeholders.

The SUI blockchain is designed to enhance the functionality and efficiency of smart contracts through its unique architecture and consensus mechanism. Unlike traditional blockchains, SUI utilizes a parallel execution model that allows for higher throughput and faster transaction times. This capability is crucial for users seeking to deploy complex decentralized applications (dApps) that can handle significant loads without compromising performance. By understanding the operational mechanics of SUI, readers can better appreciate how smart contracts are not only executed but also optimized for scalability and security.

SUI smart contracts are built using the Move programming language, which was developed to provide a secure and flexible environment for contract development. This language emphasizes safety and correctness, which are paramount when dealing with financial transactions and sensitive data. For retail investors and cryptocurrency enthusiasts, the ability to develop and interact with smart contracts on SUI opens doors to new investment opportunities and innovative financial products. The ease of creating and deploying smart contracts can empower even those with minimal technical expertise to participate in the blockchain landscape.

The implications of smart contracts extend beyond mere financial transactions; they can revolutionize various industries by automating processes and ensuring transparency. Imagine supply chain management where each step of the product journey is recorded on the blockchain, or real estate transactions that eliminate the need for lengthy paperwork. SUI's smart contracts can facilitate these applications and more, providing a framework where trust is established through code rather than human intervention. This not only enhances efficiency but also reduces the potential for fraud and errors.

In conclusion, the introduction of smart contracts on the SUI blockchain signifies a pivotal advancement in how agreements are formed and executed in a decentralized manner. As the SUI ecosystem continues to evolve, understanding the nuances of smart contracts will be essential for anyone looking to leverage this technology, whether as an investor, developer, or user of decentralized applications. By exploring the capabilities and future prospects of smart contracts on SUI, readers can position themselves at the forefront of this exciting technological frontier.

Development Tools and Frameworks

In the rapidly evolving landscape of blockchain technology, development tools and frameworks play a crucial role in enabling developers to create robust applications on the SUI blockchain. These tools are essential for building decentralized applications (dApps) and smart contracts that leverage the unique features of the SUI ecosystem. With a focus on user experience, scalability, and security, the right tools can significantly enhance the development process, making it more efficient and streamlined for both seasoned developers and newcomers to the space.

One of the primary development frameworks available for SUI is the Move programming language, which emphasizes safety and flexibility. Move is designed to facilitate the creation of secure smart contracts while minimizing common vulnerabilities associated with blockchain programming. By using this language, developers can create complex financial instruments and decentralized applications with confidence, knowing that the underlying framework has been rigorously tested for security and reliability. Additionally, the SUI blockchain's architecture, which includes native support for assets and transactions, allows developers to build applications that can interact seamlessly with the blockchain's core functionalities.

In addition to the Move language, various integrated development environments (IDEs) and tools support SUI development. These IDEs offer features like syntax highlighting, debugging capabilities, and real-time feedback, which are invaluable for improving developer productivity. Tools such as SUI CLI (Command Line Interface) enable developers to easily manage their projects, deploy contracts, and interact with the SUI blockchain. This streamlined approach not only accelerates the development process but also encourages best practices by providing a structured environment for coding and testing.

Moreover, the SUI ecosystem is complemented by a thriving community that actively contributes to the development of open-source tools and libraries. This collaboration fosters innovation and provides developers with a wealth of resources, including documentation, tutorials, and sample code. As the community continues to grow, developers can benefit from shared knowledge and experiences, which can significantly reduce the learning curve associated with blockchain development. Engaging with the community also opens up opportunities for collaboration, mentorship, and participation in governance, allowing developers to influence the direction of the SUI blockchain.

As the SUI ecosystem matures, ongoing enhancements to development tools and frameworks will be crucial for maintaining a competitive edge in the blockchain space. Continuous updates and improvements to existing tools, along with the introduction of new technologies, will empower developers to create more sophisticated applications that cater to the diverse needs of users. By leveraging these resources, developers can contribute to the broader adoption of cryptocurrencies and decentralized finance, ensuring that the SUI blockchain remains at the forefront of innovation in the industry.

Writing and Deploying Smart Contracts

Writing and deploying smart contracts on the SUI blockchain is an essential skill for anyone interested in harnessing the power of decentralized applications. Smart contracts are self-executing contracts with the terms of the agreement directly written into code. They operate on blockchain technology, ensuring transparency, security, and immutability. SUI provides a robust framework for developers to create efficient and scalable smart contracts, leveraging its unique features to enhance performance and reduce costs.

The SUI blockchain employs a programming language tailored for smart contract development, enabling developers to write contracts that are not only functional but also optimized for the SUI ecosystem. This language often emphasizes safety and simplicity, which helps mitigate common vulnerabilities associated with smart contract coding. As a developer, understanding the syntax and semantics of this programming language is crucial. Additionally, SUI's development tools and libraries facilitate the process, allowing developers to focus on logic and functionality rather than underlying complexities.

Once a smart contract is written, the next step is deploying it onto the SUI blockchain. Deployment involves uploading the contract to the network where it becomes accessible to users and other applications. SUI streamlines this process with user-friendly interfaces and comprehensive documentation, ensuring that even those new to blockchain technology can effectively deploy their contracts. It is important to conduct thorough testing in a controlled environment to ensure that the contract behaves as expected under various conditions before going live.

After deployment, smart contracts can interact with decentralized applications (dApps) on the SUI network. Developers can create dApps that utilize these contracts to offer a range of services, from financial transactions to gaming and beyond. The integration between smart contracts and dApps is seamless on the SUI blockchain, thanks to its high throughput and low latency, which are critical for user experience. This synergy not only enhances the functionality of individual applications but also contributes to the overall growth of the SUI ecosystem.

Understanding the importance of security in smart contract development cannot be overstated. The immutable nature of blockchain means that once a contract is deployed, it cannot be altered. Therefore, developers must adhere to best practices for coding and auditing their smart contracts. SUI emphasizes community involvement in security practices, encouraging developers to share knowledge and tools for auditing and testing. By fostering a collaborative environment, SUI aims to minimize vulnerabilities and enhance the reliability of smart contracts across the network, making it a trusted platform for both developers and users.

Best Practices for Smart Contract Development

When developing smart contracts on the SUI blockchain, adhering to best practices is crucial for ensuring security, efficiency, and reliability. One of the foundational principles is to write clear and concise code. Smart contracts often handle significant assets and complex logic, making it essential that the code is easily understandable and well-documented. This clarity not only facilitates easier audits but also helps future developers who may work on the contract. Employing descriptive variable and function names can greatly enhance the readability of the code, reducing the chances of misunderstandings and errors during development.

Testing is another critical aspect of smart contract development. A comprehensive testing strategy should include unit tests, integration tests, and simulation of various attack vectors to identify vulnerabilities. Utilizing test networks allows developers to deploy their contracts in a safe environment before moving to the mainnet. Developers should also consider employing formal verification methods, which mathematically prove the correctness of the contract's logic. This additional layer of scrutiny can help prevent costly mistakes that could arise from overlooked bugs or flaws in the contract.

Security audits are an indispensable part of the smart contract development process. Engaging third-party auditors who specialize in blockchain technology can provide an objective evaluation of the contract. These audits help uncover potential security loopholes and design flaws that the original developers may have missed. It is advisable to incorporate feedback from these audits into the final version of the smart contract before deployment. Additionally, maintaining a bug bounty program post-launch can incentivize external developers to identify and report vulnerabilities, fostering a culture of continuous improvement and vigilance.

Employing best practices in version control and project management is equally important for the successful development of smart contracts. Using platforms like Git allows developers to track changes, collaborate efficiently, and maintain a history of modifications made to the contract. Versioning helps in managing updates and ensuring that any changes are well-documented and reversible if necessary. Furthermore, utilizing agile methodologies can streamline the development process, allowing teams to adapt to new challenges and requirements quickly while maintaining a focus on delivering a high-quality product.

Lastly, staying informed about the evolving landscape of blockchain technology and smart contracts is vital for developers. Regularly engaging with the SUI community can provide insights into new tools, techniques, and best practices that can enhance development efforts. Participating in forums, attending workshops, or contributing to open-source projects can foster a deeper understanding of the ecosystem. By being proactive in learning and adapting, developers can ensure that their smart contracts not only meet current standards but are also prepared for future advancements in the SUI blockchain and beyond.

Chapter 4: SUI Decentralized Applications (dApps)

Overview of dApps on the SUI Blockchain

The SUI blockchain represents a significant evolution in decentralized applications, or dApps, offering unique features that enhance usability and functionality. dApps on SUI are built with a focus on scalability and efficiency, utilizing a novel architecture that allows for high throughput and low latency. This means that users can engage with applications without the frustration of slow transaction times or network congestion, which are common issues in other blockchain networks. The user experience is further enhanced by SUI's ability to support complex operations, making it an attractive option for developers and businesses aiming to create innovative solutions.

One of the standout characteristics of dApps on the SUI blockchain is their flexibility in design and functionality. Developers can leverage SUI's smart contract capabilities to create a wide array of applications, from financial services to social platforms. This versatility is crucial for fostering a diverse ecosystem where various sectors can explore blockchain integration. The SUI ecosystem encourages experimentation, enabling developers to implement novel concepts and features that cater to specific user needs and market demands.

Security is a paramount concern in the blockchain space, and SUI addresses this with robust protocols that protect both users and developers. dApps on the SUI blockchain benefit from state-of-the-art security measures, ensuring that transactions are secure and data integrity is maintained. The incorporation of best practices in smart contract development and regular audits further bolsters user confidence, making SUI an appealing platform for those wary of potential vulnerabilities that can arise in the decentralized space.

Community involvement is also a cornerstone of the SUI blockchain's dApp ecosystem. The community actively participates in governance, providing feedback and suggestions that shape the development of applications and protocols. This collaborative spirit not only enhances the quality of dApps but also fosters a sense of ownership among users. As the community grows, so does the potential for innovative solutions and improvements, creating a dynamic environment that benefits all stakeholders.

Looking ahead, the roadmap for dApps on the SUI blockchain is promising, with ongoing developments aimed at expanding functionality and accessibility. As more developers and users engage with the ecosystem, the potential for widespread adoption increases. Retail investors and cryptocurrency enthusiasts can look forward to a robust array of applications that not only offer investment opportunities but also enhance everyday activities through decentralized solutions. The future of dApps on SUI is bright, positioning the platform as a key player in the evolving landscape of blockchain technology.

Popular dApps in the SUI Ecosystem

The SUI ecosystem has rapidly gained traction within the blockchain community, particularly due to its innovative decentralized applications (dApps) that cater to a diverse range of users, including retail investors and cryptocurrency enthusiasts. Among the most notable dApps in this ecosystem are those focused on decentralized finance (DeFi), gaming, and non-fungible tokens (NFTs). These applications leverage the unique features of the SUI blockchain, such as its high throughput and low latency, to provide seamless experiences that attract both new and seasoned users.

One of the standout dApps in the SUI ecosystem is SUI Finance, a decentralized lending and borrowing platform that allows users to take advantage of their crypto assets. By enabling users to earn interest on their holdings or access liquidity without selling their assets, SUI Finance exemplifies the core principles of DeFi. Its user-friendly interface and robust security measures have made it a popular choice among retail investors looking to maximize their returns while minimizing risk. The platform's integration with various cryptocurrencies further enhances its appeal, as users can diversify their portfolios within a single dApp.

In the realm of gaming, SUI Play has emerged as a leading dApp, offering a variety of play-to-earn games that reward users for their time and skill. With a strong emphasis on community engagement and user-generated content, SUI Play fosters a vibrant ecosystem where players can not only enjoy immersive gaming experiences but also earn cryptocurrency rewards. This model has resonated particularly well with meme coin enthusiasts, who often seek entertaining and interactive ways to engage with the crypto space. The success of SUI Play highlights the potential of gamification in driving user adoption and retention within the SUI ecosystem.

Another significant dApp is SUI Art, a marketplace for non-fungible tokens that allows artists and creators to tokenize their work and connect directly with collectors. SUI Art has positioned itself as a go-to platform for digital artists, providing them with the tools to showcase their creations while ensuring secure transactions through the use of smart contracts. The platform's focus on community-driven initiatives, such as auctions and collaborations, has fostered a supportive environment where creativity can flourish. This has attracted a diverse audience, including both seasoned collectors and new investors looking to explore the world of digital art.

As the SUI ecosystem continues to evolve, the development of these popular dApps illustrates the potential for innovation within the blockchain space. With a robust framework for smart contracts, a commitment to security, and a growing community of users and developers, SUI is well-positioned to capitalize on emerging trends in the cryptocurrency market. Whether through DeFi solutions, engaging gaming experiences, or vibrant NFT marketplaces, the SUI ecosystem is paving the way for a future where decentralized applications play a central role in the lives of cryptocurrency enthusiasts and investors alike.

Developing dApps on SUI

Developing decentralized applications (dApps) on the SUI blockchain offers a unique opportunity for creators to build innovative solutions tailored to the needs of users in the cryptocurrency space. SUI's architecture is designed for scalability and efficiency, making it an attractive platform for developers looking to tap into the growing demand for decentralized services. With its focus on user experience, SUI supports the creation of dApps that can cater to both seasoned crypto enthusiasts and newcomers alike, facilitating engagement across diverse segments of the cryptocurrency market.

The SUI blockchain employs a novel data modeling system that allows developers to leverage its capabilities without extensive overhead. This system supports a wide array of programming languages, enabling developers to utilize familiar tools and frameworks while building their dApps. The ease of integration with existing tools and libraries accelerates the development process, allowing teams to focus on innovation rather than grappling with complex infrastructure. Consequently, those interested in cryptocurrencies can expect a variety of user-friendly applications that enhance their interaction with digital assets.

Security remains a paramount concern in the world of dApp development, and SUI addresses this by implementing robust security protocols. The platform's architecture includes built-in features that help safeguard against common vulnerabilities, ensuring that applications are resilient to threats. Developers are encouraged to adopt best practices in security when creating their dApps, such as regular audits and employing decentralized identity verification methods. By prioritizing security, SUI fosters a trustworthy environment where users can engage confidently with decentralized applications.

In addition to security, community involvement plays a critical role in the dApp development process on SUI. The SUI community is active and engaged, providing valuable feedback and resources for developers. This collaborative spirit is essential for creating applications that genuinely meet user needs and preferences. Developers can leverage community insights to refine their dApps and enhance their functionality, ultimately contributing to a more vibrant ecosystem that benefits all participants, from retail investors to meme coin enthusiasts.

Looking ahead, the roadmap for SUI includes initiatives aimed at expanding its dApp ecosystem further. With ongoing enhancements to the platform's capabilities and a commitment to fostering innovation, developers have a promising landscape in which to create. As the SUI ecosystem continues to grow, it will likely attract a diverse range of applications across various industries, solidifying its position as a leading blockchain for decentralized applications. Retail investors and cryptocurrency enthusiasts can anticipate a wealth of opportunities as more dApps emerge, driving the adoption of blockchain technology in everyday transactions and interactions.

User Experience and Interface Design Considerations

User experience (UX) and interface design are critical components in the development of decentralized applications (dApps) within the SUI ecosystem. With the growing interest in cryptocurrencies and the rise of meme coins, it is essential to create an engaging and intuitive user interface that caters to both seasoned investors and newcomers. A well-designed interface not only enhances usability but also fosters trust and confidence in the application, which is particularly vital in the context of financial transactions and investment decisions.

When designing a user interface for SUI-based applications, developers must consider the diverse backgrounds of their target audience. Retail investors and meme coin enthusiasts often seek quick access to information, streamlined navigation, and visually appealing aesthetics. Simplicity should be a guiding principle; a cluttered interface can overwhelm users, leading to frustration and potential disengagement. Therefore, using clear icons, concise labels, and a logical flow can significantly enhance the user experience, making it easier for individuals to navigate through complex blockchain functionalities.

Another important aspect of UX design in the SUI ecosystem is the integration of educational elements. Many users may be unfamiliar with blockchain technology, smart contracts, or the specific features of SUI. Providing tooltips, tutorials, or onboarding guides can help demystify these concepts. This educational approach not only empowers users but also encourages greater participation in the SUI community by fostering a deeper understanding of the technology behind the applications they are using.

Accessibility is also a key consideration in the design of SUI applications. Ensuring that interfaces are usable by individuals with varying levels of ability enhances inclusivity. This can involve implementing features such as adjustable text sizes, high-contrast modes, and screen reader compatibility. By prioritizing accessibility, developers can reach a broader audience and create a more equitable environment within the cryptocurrency space, where all users can engage with the technology effectively.

Finally, continuous feedback and iteration are vital in refining the user experience. Engaging the community through surveys, usability testing, and feedback sessions allows developers to identify pain points and areas for improvement. By actively involving users in the design process, applications can evolve to meet the changing needs and preferences of the community. In the fast-paced world of cryptocurrencies, where trends and technologies are constantly evolving, maintaining an adaptive approach in UX and interface design will be essential for the long-term success of SUI applications.

Chapter 5: SUI Governance and Community Involvement

Understanding SUI Governance Models

Understanding SUI governance models is crucial for anyone navigating the multifaceted landscape of the SUI ecosystem. Governance in the context of blockchain refers to the mechanisms and processes through which decisions are made regarding the network's operation, development, and evolution. SUI, as a blockchain technology, incorporates various governance models that aim to engage the community while ensuring transparency and efficiency. By understanding these models, investors and enthusiasts can better appreciate how their participation influences the SUI network's trajectory.

One of the primary governance models utilized in SUI is the decentralized autonomous organization (DAO). DAOs enable token holders to participate directly in decision-making processes, allowing them to vote on proposals that affect the network. This democratic approach empowers users and ensures that the governance structure is aligned with the community's interests. As SUI continues to grow, the importance of DAOs in facilitating active participation cannot be overstated, making them essential for retail investors and crypto enthusiasts looking to have a say in the platform's future.

Another notable model within the SUI governance framework is the delegation mechanism. This system allows token holders to delegate their voting power to representatives or experts within the community. This is particularly beneficial for those who may not have the time or expertise to engage in every aspect of governance. By enabling a more streamlined decision-making process, delegation fosters a more inclusive environment where diverse voices can still be represented. This becomes increasingly significant as the SUI ecosystem expands and the number of proposals grows.

The SUI governance model also emphasizes transparency and accountability through regular reporting and community engagement initiatives. By maintaining open lines of communication about governance decisions and their implications, the SUI community can build trust among its members. This transparency is vital for retail investors and meme coin enthusiasts, who often seek assurance that their investments are being managed responsibly and in alignment with community values. Furthermore, active community involvement in governance discussions not only enhances decision-making but also strengthens the overall ecosystem.

In conclusion, understanding the various governance models within the SUI ecosystem is essential for anyone interested in cryptocurrency, including retail investors and meme coin enthusiasts. The integration of DAOs, delegation mechanisms, and a commitment to transparency ensures that the SUI network remains adaptable and responsive to the needs of its community. By engaging with these governance structures, individuals can play an active role in shaping the future of SUI, making it a more vibrant and inclusive environment for all participants.

Role of the Community in Decision-Making

In the evolving landscape of blockchain technology, the role of the community in decision-making processes is paramount, particularly within the SUI ecosystem. Communities drive the ethos of decentralization, ensuring that the development and governance of the SUI blockchain are not solely in the hands of a few developers or stakeholders. Instead, they empower users, investors, and enthusiasts to voice their opinions, propose changes, and participate actively in the decision-making processes that shape the future of the platform. This collaborative approach helps to cultivate a robust ecosystem that is responsive to the needs and desires of its users.

Community involvement is a critical component of SUI governance, where members often engage in discussions through forums, social media platforms, and governance voting mechanisms. These channels allow for a diverse range of perspectives to be heard, fostering an environment where innovative ideas can flourish. The SUI community can propose enhancements to the blockchain, vote on protocol upgrades, and set the direction for future developments. This participatory framework not only enhances transparency but also builds trust among community members, encouraging them to contribute actively to the ecosystem.

Moreover, the decentralized nature of decision-making within SUI allows for a more democratic process, reducing the risk of centralization that can plague other blockchain projects. This is particularly appealing to retail investors and meme coin enthusiasts, who often seek platforms that prioritize community input and equitable participation. By placing decision-making power in the hands of the community, SUI can attract a wider audience, ensuring that the interests of both small and large stakeholders are considered. This inclusivity is essential for fostering a loyal and engaged user base that is invested in the success of the platform.

The impact of community-driven decision-making extends beyond governance; it also influences the development of decentralized applications (dApps) within the SUI ecosystem. Developers are encouraged to build solutions that address the specific needs and preferences expressed by the community. This collaborative model not only enhances the relevance of the dApps created but also encourages innovation as developers leverage community feedback to refine their projects. As a result, the SUI ecosystem becomes a vibrant space for experimentation and growth, with applications tailored to the desires of its users.

In conclusion, the role of the community in decision-making within the SUI ecosystem is fundamental to its growth and success. By fostering an inclusive and participatory environment, SUI not only empowers its users but also ensures that the platform evolves in a manner that aligns with the collective vision of its community members. As cryptocurrencies and blockchain technology continue to advance, the importance of community involvement in shaping these innovations will only become more pronounced, solidifying the foundation upon which the SUI ecosystem is built.

Participating in Governance Proposals

Participating in governance proposals is a fundamental aspect of the SUI ecosystem, enabling users to engage actively in the decision-making processes that shape the platform's future. Governance within SUI is designed to be inclusive, allowing stakeholders, including retail investors and meme coin enthusiasts, to have a say in the direction of the project. The decentralized nature of this governance means that every voice can contribute to discussions about protocol upgrades, community initiatives, and resource allocation, fostering a sense of ownership among participants.

To get involved, users must first understand how governance proposals are structured within the SUI framework. Proposals typically originate from community members or developers who identify areas for improvement or new features that could enhance the ecosystem. Once a proposal is formulated, it goes through a review process where it is discussed among community members. This phase is crucial, as it allows for feedback and iterations, ensuring that the final proposal aligns with the community's needs and expectations.

Voting on governance proposals is another critical component of this process. SUI employs a token-based voting mechanism, where users can cast their votes using SUI tokens. The weight of a user's vote is proportional to the number of tokens they hold, giving significant stakeholders a more substantial influence on the outcomes. However, this does not diminish the importance of smaller holders, as collective voting power can be mobilized to effect change. Engaging in voting is vital, as it directly impacts the governance of the ecosystem and the implementation of proposals.

Participation extends beyond mere voting; community engagement happens through forums, social media channels, and governance platforms where discussions take place. These platforms serve as vital communication channels for users to voice their opinions, share insights, and collaborate on proposals. Active participation in these discussions can lead to a more refined understanding of the ecosystem's needs and challenges. Furthermore, it allows users to network with like-minded individuals, building a community of passionate supporters who can drive initiatives forward.

Finally, the ongoing evolution of governance proposals reflects the dynamic nature of the SUI ecosystem. As the technology and community grow, so too do the mechanisms for governance. Users are encouraged to stay informed about ongoing discussions, upcoming votes, and the broader implications of each proposal. By actively participating in governance proposals, individuals not only contribute to shaping the SUI ecosystem but also enhance their own understanding of blockchain governance, making them more informed investors and engaged community members.

Building and Sustaining Community Engagement

Building and sustaining community engagement is essential for the growth and success of any ecosystem, particularly within the SUI framework. In the world of cryptocurrencies and blockchain technology, community plays a pivotal role in driving innovation, adoption, and overall value. The SUI ecosystem thrives on active participation from its members, which includes developers, investors, and enthusiasts. Engaging with the community fosters a sense of belonging and encourages collaboration, ultimately leading to the creation of decentralized applications (dApps) that meet user needs and enhance the overall functionality of the SUI blockchain.

To build a thriving community, it is crucial to leverage multiple channels of communication. Social media platforms, forums, and dedicated chat groups serve as vital spaces where individuals can share insights, ask questions, and provide feedback. Regular updates on the SUI roadmap, technology advancements, and governance decisions should be communicated transparently to keep the community informed and involved. By fostering open dialogue, the SUI ecosystem can cultivate a culture of trust and respect, which is fundamental for sustainable engagement. Moreover, hosting webinars, AMAs (Ask Me Anything sessions), and online meetups can further facilitate interaction and knowledge sharing among community members.

In addition to communication, providing educational resources is vital for community engagement. Many individuals interested in cryptocurrencies may have varying levels of understanding about blockchain technology and its applications. By offering tutorials, guides, and workshops focused on SUI smart contracts, development practices, and security protocols, the ecosystem can empower users to participate meaningfully. Educational initiatives not only enhance the skill sets of community members but also inspire confidence in the SUI technology. As a result, this can lead to increased participation in governance, development, and investment activities within the ecosystem.

Sustaining community engagement requires ongoing recognition and appreciation of contributions from members. Acknowledging the efforts of developers who create innovative dApps or investors who support the ecosystem can significantly enhance motivation and commitment. Implementing reward systems, such as token incentives or recognition programs, can further encourage active participation. Additionally, fostering inclusivity by welcoming diverse perspectives and encouraging collaboration across different niches can lead to richer discussions and more innovative solutions within the SUI community.

Lastly, it is essential to gather feedback and adapt to the evolving needs of the community. Establishing mechanisms for collecting input, such as surveys or feedback forms, allows the SUI ecosystem to remain responsive to its members. This adaptability not only strengthens community ties but also ensures that the development of SUI technologies remains aligned with user expectations and industry trends. By prioritizing community engagement through effective communication, education, recognition, and adaptability, the SUI ecosystem can thrive, driving both innovation and user satisfaction in the ever-evolving landscape of cryptocurrency and blockchain technology.

Chapter 6: SUI Security Protocols and Best Practices

Overview of Security in Blockchain

The security of blockchain technology is a foundational aspect that underpins its appeal to cryptocurrency enthusiasts, retail investors, and the broader community. At its core, blockchain is designed to be secure, leveraging cryptographic techniques to ensure that data is immutable and transactions are transparent. Each block in a blockchain contains a cryptographic hash of the previous block, creating a chain that is extremely difficult to alter without detection. This feature not only protects against fraud but also builds trust among users by ensuring that once data is recorded, it cannot be easily tampered with.

One of the most significant security features of blockchain is decentralization. Unlike traditional financial systems that rely on a central authority, blockchain operates on a distributed network of nodes that validate transactions. This reduces the risk of a single point of failure and makes it much more challenging for malicious actors to compromise the system. In the context of SUI, this decentralized approach enhances security by allowing a diverse group of participants to partake in the validation process, thus ensuring that no single entity can gain control over the network.

Smart contracts, which are self-executing agreements coded into the blockchain, also play a crucial role in enhancing security. By automating processes and reducing the need for intermediaries, smart contracts minimize the risk of human error and potential fraud. However, it is essential for developers to follow best practices in coding these contracts to avoid vulnerabilities. In the SUI ecosystem, a focus on robust smart contract development can help mitigate risks associated with bugs and exploits, ensuring that decentralized applications (dApps) operate as intended.

Despite these inherent security features, blockchain is not immune to threats. Risks such as hacking, phishing, and social engineering attacks can still pose significant challenges. For instance, if users do not practice proper security hygiene, such as safeguarding their private keys, they may fall victim to theft. Moreover, as the SUI ecosystem evolves, it is crucial for the community to stay informed about emerging threats and adopt proactive measures to safeguard their assets. Engaging in community discussions and participating in governance can lead to the implementation of effective security protocols.

To summarize, understanding the security landscape of blockchain, particularly within the SUI framework, is vital for anyone involved in cryptocurrencies. The combination of decentralized validation, cryptographic techniques, and smart contracts provides a robust foundation for security. However, users must remain vigilant and informed to navigate the evolving threats and challenges. By fostering a culture of security awareness and community involvement, the SUI ecosystem can enhance its resilience against potential risks, ensuring a safer environment for all participants.

Security Features of the SUI Blockchain

The SUI blockchain incorporates a robust array of security features designed to protect users and their assets while ensuring the integrity of transactions. One of the foundational elements of SUI's security is its use of a proof-of-stake consensus mechanism. By requiring validators to stake a certain amount of SUI tokens, the network discourages malicious behaviors, as any attempt to compromise the blockchain would result in a financial loss for the validator. This not only enhances the security of the network but also fosters a sense of responsibility among participants, as their financial interests are directly tied to the network's performance.

Another crucial aspect of SUI's security architecture is its multi-layered approach to data integrity and verification. The blockchain employs cryptographic techniques to ensure that all transactions are securely recorded and immutable. This means that once a transaction is confirmed, it cannot be altered or deleted without the consensus of the network. Such immutability protects users from fraud and provides a transparent history of all transactions, bolstering trust among participants. The implementation of advanced hashing algorithms further fortifies this process by ensuring that any changes to transaction data would be immediately evident to the network.

In addition to these foundational security measures, SUI also prioritizes user privacy through the integration of advanced privacy protocols. These protocols allow users to conduct transactions without revealing their identities, thereby protecting sensitive information from potential threats. By utilizing techniques such as zero-knowledge proofs, SUI ensures that while transaction validity is maintained, the details remain confidential. This is particularly appealing to retail investors and cryptocurrency enthusiasts who value anonymity and security in their financial dealings.

Smart contracts on the SUI platform are designed with security in mind as well. The platform employs rigorous testing and auditing practices to identify and mitigate vulnerabilities before contracts are deployed. This proactive stance minimizes the risk of exploits that can lead to significant financial losses. Additionally, SUI encourages developers to follow best practices and utilize established frameworks for smart contract development, further enhancing the overall security of the ecosystem. The emphasis on secure coding practices and thorough audits builds confidence among users and developers alike.

Lastly, the SUI community plays an integral role in maintaining the security of the blockchain. Active community involvement helps identify potential security threats and fosters a culture of vigilance.

Through governance mechanisms, users can propose and vote on security enhancements, ensuring that the network evolves in response to emerging risks. This collaborative approach not only empowers users but also creates a resilient and adaptive security framework that can withstand the ever-changing landscape of the cryptocurrency market. By prioritizing security at every level, SUI positions itself as a trustworthy and reliable platform for all participants in the blockchain ecosystem.

Common Vulnerabilities and Threats

The landscape of cryptocurrencies is riddled with various vulnerabilities and threats that can significantly impact both individual investors and the broader ecosystem. One common vulnerability is the susceptibility to phishing attacks, where malicious actors trick users into revealing their private keys or sensitive information through deceptive emails or websites. This type of threat is particularly concerning for those involved in the SUI ecosystem, as it can lead to significant financial losses. Investors must remain vigilant and educate themselves on identifying phishing attempts to safeguard their assets.

Another prevalent threat is the exploitation of smart contracts, which are integral to the functionality of decentralized applications (dApps) within the SUI framework. Vulnerabilities in smart contract coding can be exploited by attackers, leading to unauthorized transactions or the draining of funds. The infamous hacks of various DeFi projects serve as cautionary tales for both developers and users. It is essential for those engaging with SUI smart contracts to understand the importance of rigorous testing and audits, ensuring that their applications are secure before deployment.

In addition to phishing and smart contract vulnerabilities, the threat of network attacks cannot be overlooked. Distributed Denial of Service (DDoS) attacks are designed to overwhelm a network's resources, rendering dApps inoperable and resulting in loss of access for users. Such attacks can undermine trust in the SUI ecosystem and deter potential investors. Proactive measures, including the implementation of robust security protocols and monitoring tools, are critical for maintaining the integrity and availability of SUI-based applications.

Moreover, the evolving regulatory landscape poses a unique challenge to cryptocurrency platforms, including those within the SUI ecosystem. Potential changes in legislation can create uncertainty, affecting investor confidence and market dynamics. Retail investors must stay informed about regulatory developments and understand how these changes could impact their investments in SUI and other cryptocurrencies. Engaging with community discussions and governance mechanisms can provide insights into how these threats are being addressed collectively.

Finally, the rise of social engineering tactics in the cryptocurrency space, particularly among meme coin enthusiasts, highlights another layer of vulnerability. Scammers often exploit the enthusiasm surrounding trending coins to promote fraudulent schemes, leading unsuspecting investors to lose their money. Education and awareness are vital in combating these threats, as investors must critically evaluate projects before investing. By fostering a culture of vigilance and sharing knowledge within the SUI community, individuals can better protect themselves and contribute to a more secure cryptocurrency environment.

Best Practices for Ensuring Security

Ensuring security within the SUI ecosystem is paramount for anyone engaging with cryptocurrencies, especially for retail investors and enthusiasts of meme coins. The decentralized nature of blockchain technology provides a robust framework, but it also introduces unique vulnerabilities that can be exploited if not properly addressed. Adopting best practices for security is essential to protect investments and foster trust in the SUI ecosystem. Users must prioritize understanding potential threats and implementing measures to mitigate risks associated with their digital assets.

One of the fundamental best practices is the use of secure wallets. Hardware wallets, for instance, offer an excellent layer of security by storing private keys offline, making them less susceptible to hacking attempts compared to software wallets. Additionally, users should regularly update their wallet software to incorporate the latest security features and patches. For those utilizing hot wallets for convenience, it is critical to implement strong passwords and enable two-factor authentication to add an extra layer of protection against unauthorized access.

Another critical aspect of security in the SUI ecosystem involves being vigilant about phishing attacks. Cybercriminals often employ deceptive tactics to trick users into revealing sensitive information or accessing malicious sites. It is essential for users to verify the authenticity of websites and links before interacting with them. Bookmarking frequently used addresses and utilizing browser extensions that flag suspicious sites can significantly reduce the risk of falling victim to phishing schemes. Furthermore, educating oneself on common phishing tactics can empower users to recognize potential threats more effectively.

Smart contracts, which play a vital role in the SUI ecosystem, also require careful scrutiny. Users should prioritize transparency and auditability when interacting with smart contracts. Engaging with projects that have undergone third-party security audits can help ensure that the code is robust and free from vulnerabilities. Additionally, understanding the terms and conditions of the contract, including any potential risks, is crucial before committing any assets. This due diligence can significantly enhance security and safeguard against potential exploits.

Lastly, community involvement and governance participation can play a significant role in enhancing security within the SUI ecosystem. By actively engaging with the community, users can stay informed about emerging threats and best practices. Participating in discussions regarding security improvements and reporting vulnerabilities can help create a more resilient environment for all users. Collective vigilance and proactive measures within the community not only strengthen individual security but also contribute to the overall integrity of the SUI ecosystem, promoting a safer space for cryptocurrency engagement.

Chapter 7: SUI Use Cases in Various Industries

Financial Services and Banking

Financial services and banking have undergone a significant transformation with the advent of blockchain technology, particularly through the innovations presented by the SUI ecosystem. Traditional banking, often characterized by centralized control and lengthy transaction processes, is being challenged by decentralized financial services (DeFi) that offer greater transparency, efficiency, and accessibility. The SUI blockchain, with its advanced architecture and smart contract capabilities, provides a robust platform for creating financial applications that can streamline lending, borrowing, and asset management while reducing the costs typically associated with traditional banking.

One of the most notable applications of SUI in financial services is its ability to facilitate peer-to-peer transactions without the need for intermediaries. This capability dramatically lowers the barriers to entry for individuals looking to participate in the financial system. Retail investors, in particular, can benefit from SUI's decentralized applications (dApps) that enable them to trade, invest, and manage their portfolios in a secure environment. By leveraging the SUI blockchain, users can execute transactions almost instantaneously, enhancing their trading strategies and investment opportunities.

Moreover, the SUI ecosystem promotes financial inclusion by providing access to banking services for unbanked populations. With SUI's user-friendly interfaces and decentralized applications, individuals in regions with limited banking infrastructure can easily participate in the global economy. This opens up opportunities for microloans, savings accounts, and even insurance products, all of which can be managed through smart contracts on the SUI blockchain, ensuring that users maintain control over their assets while benefiting from the innovations of DeFi.

The governance model within the SUI ecosystem also plays a vital role in shaping financial services. Community involvement in decision-making processes ensures that the development of financial products aligns with the needs and interests of users. This participatory approach fosters a sense of ownership and encourages the creation of services that are not only innovative but also responsible and sustainable. As the SUI community continues to grow, the collaborative development of DeFi solutions will likely lead to new financial products tailored to specific user needs, enhancing the overall utility of the ecosystem.

Security is a paramount concern in financial services, and the SUI blockchain addresses this with its advanced security protocols. By utilizing cryptographic techniques and decentralized verification processes, SUI ensures that transactions are not only secure but also tamper-proof. Retail investors can engage with financial services with confidence, knowing that their assets and data are protected. As the SUI ecosystem evolves, continuous improvements in security measures will be essential for maintaining trust and encouraging broader adoption of decentralized financial applications among users who are increasingly wary of traditional banking systems.

Supply Chain Management

Supply chain management (SCM) is a critical aspect of modern commerce, and the advent of blockchain technology has introduced transformative potential in this domain. In the context of SUI, SCM can leverage decentralized applications to enhance transparency, efficiency, and trust between parties involved in the supply chain. By utilizing SUI's blockchain capabilities, businesses can monitor and manage their supply chains in real time, reducing the risks associated with fraud and errors while ensuring that all participants have access to accurate and up-to-date information.

One of the primary advantages of implementing SCM on the SUI blockchain is the inherent transparency that comes with decentralized ledgers. Each transaction or movement of goods can be recorded immutably, providing an auditable trail that stakeholders can trust. Retail investors and cryptocurrency enthusiasts can appreciate how this transparency minimizes disputes and enhances accountability, leading to a more reliable supply chain. This is particularly beneficial for industries where provenance is critical, such as food and pharmaceuticals, where consumers demand assurance about the origins and handling of products.

Smart contracts play a pivotal role in automating processes within supply chain management on the SUI blockchain. These self-executing contracts facilitate transactions when certain conditions are met, effectively reducing the need for intermediaries and streamlining operations. For meme coin enjoyers and those invested in the SUI ecosystem, understanding smart contracts' functionality can provide insights into how they can be utilized to optimize logistics, payments, and compliance throughout the supply chain. This automation not only accelerates processes but also lowers operational costs, making businesses more competitive.

The SUI ecosystem also supports the development of decentralized applications (dApps) tailored for supply chain management. These dApps can enable real-time tracking of inventory, order processing, and shipment monitoring, offering a holistic view of the supply chain. As retail investors seek innovative projects within the cryptocurrency space, they should consider the potential impact of such dApps on traditional supply chains. By addressing common inefficiencies, these applications can significantly enhance customer satisfaction and foster loyalty through improved service delivery.

Looking ahead, the future developments of supply chain management within the SUI ecosystem are promising. As organizations increasingly recognize the value of blockchain technology, the adoption of SUI for SCM could lead to more sustainable practices, reduced waste, and an overall increase in supply chain resilience. The roadmap for SUI indicates a commitment to enhancing its capabilities, which will enable businesses and investors alike to harness the power of blockchain for more robust and responsible supply chain solutions. As this technology continues to evolve, stakeholders will benefit from a more connected and efficient global marketplace.

Healthcare Applications

Healthcare applications of blockchain technology, particularly those built on the SUI platform, present a transformative potential for the industry. With the growing complexity of healthcare systems, the need for secure, efficient, and transparent data management has never been more critical. SUI's unique architecture allows for the creation of decentralized applications (dApps) that can streamline processes such as patient data sharing, medical record management, and the secure transfer of sensitive information. By leveraging SUI's smart contracts, healthcare providers can automate workflows, reducing administrative burdens and improving patient care outcomes.

One of the key advantages of utilizing SUI in healthcare is the enhancement of data interoperability. Traditional healthcare systems often suffer from fragmented data silos, making it difficult for different providers to access and share information. SUI's blockchain enables a unified protocol for data exchange, ensuring that patient records are accessible yet secure. This interoperability allows for seamless collaboration among healthcare professionals, ultimately leading to improved diagnostic accuracy and treatment efficacy. Patients benefit as well, as they gain more control over their health data and can grant access to providers on a need-to-know basis.

Additionally, SUI's governance model fosters community involvement, which is crucial in the healthcare sector. By implementing decentralized governance, stakeholders, including patients, healthcare providers, and researchers, can participate in decision-making processes. This collaborative approach not only increases transparency but also ensures that the development of healthcare applications aligns with the needs and preferences of the community. The SUI ecosystem encourages ongoing dialogue and feedback, leading to continuously evolving solutions that better serve the healthcare landscape.

Security is another paramount consideration in healthcare applications. SUI's robust security protocols protect sensitive patient information against breaches and unauthorized access. The use of cryptographic techniques ensures that data remains confidential and tamper-proof, instilling trust among users. Healthcare organizations can confidently adopt SUI-based solutions, knowing that they comply with regulatory requirements and maintain the integrity of their data. This trust is essential as patients become more vigilant about their privacy and seek assurances that their information is handled responsibly.

In conclusion, the integration of SUI blockchain technology within healthcare applications offers a promising pathway to enhance efficiency, security, and patient empowerment. As the healthcare industry continues to embrace digital transformation, the versatility of SUI will enable innovative solutions that address longstanding challenges. By harnessing the power of decentralized technology, stakeholders can work together to create a more connected and resilient healthcare ecosystem, ultimately leading to better health outcomes for individuals and communities alike.

Gaming and Entertainment

Gaming and entertainment have emerged as significant frontiers within the SUI ecosystem, harnessing the power of blockchain technology to create immersive experiences that transcend traditional barriers. The integration of cryptocurrencies into gaming platforms has redefined how players engage with their favorite titles, allowing for true ownership of in-game assets through non-fungible tokens (NFTs) and enabling seamless transactions via digital currencies. The SUI blockchain's unique architecture supports high throughput and low latency, which are essential for real-time gaming applications, ensuring players enjoy a seamless experience without the lag often associated with decentralized platforms.

One of the most exciting developments in this space is the rise of play-to-earn models, where players can earn cryptocurrency rewards by participating in games. This paradigm shift not only incentivizes player engagement but also creates economic opportunities within the gaming community. SUI's smart contracts facilitate these transactions, ensuring transparent and secure distribution of rewards. Moreover, game developers are increasingly turning to SUI to build decentralized applications (dApps) that allow for innovative gameplay mechanics, such as player-driven economies and governance models that empower users to influence game development and direction.

The SUI ecosystem also encourages collaboration between developers and gamers, fostering a community-centric approach to game design. With governance mechanisms in place, players can voice their opinions on updates, new features, and in-game policies, creating a sense of ownership and involvement that is rarely seen in traditional gaming. This community engagement not only enhances user experience but also drives the continuous evolution of games, ensuring they remain relevant and enjoyable over time.

Security remains a paramount concern in the gaming industry, particularly when financial transactions are involved. SUI's robust security protocols are designed to protect users from fraud and hacking, providing a safe environment for gamers to engage with their digital assets. By implementing best practices for security, SUI ensures that players can focus on enjoyment and competition without the looming fear of losing their investments. This commitment to security helps to build trust within the gaming community, which is crucial for the long-term success of any blockchain-based entertainment platform.

As the gaming and entertainment landscape continues to evolve, the SUI ecosystem is poised to play a pivotal role in shaping the future of digital interactions. With ongoing developments and a clear roadmap for future enhancements, SUI is not only addressing current challenges but also exploring new avenues for innovation in gaming. From enhancing user experiences to expanding the potential for earnings, SUI is set to redefine the interplay between entertainment and blockchain technology, making it an exciting time for investors and gamers alike.

Chapter 8: SUI Roadmap and Future Developments

Current Status of the SUI Blockchain

The current status of the SUI blockchain reflects a dynamic ecosystem that is rapidly evolving to meet the needs of various stakeholders within the cryptocurrency community. Since its inception, SUI has positioned itself as a high-performance layer-1 blockchain, designed to facilitate fast transactions and support a wide range of decentralized applications (dApps). Its architecture leverages a unique move semantics programming model, enhancing the efficiency and security of smart contracts. This innovative approach not only attracts developers looking to build powerful dApps but also appeals to retail investors and meme coin enthusiasts seeking promising investment opportunities.

As of now, the SUI blockchain has garnered significant attention due to its scalability and low-latency transaction capabilities. With the increasing demand for decentralized finance (DeFi) applications and non-fungible tokens (NFTs), SUI's infrastructure is well-suited to handle high volumes of transactions without compromising speed or security. This robust performance has led to partnerships with various projects and platforms, further solidifying SUI's position in the competitive blockchain landscape. The active development community continuously works to enhance the platform, ensuring it remains at the forefront of technological advancements.

In terms of governance, SUI emphasizes community involvement, allowing stakeholders to participate in key decision-making processes. This decentralized governance model not only empowers users but also fosters a sense of ownership and accountability within the ecosystem. Regular community discussions, proposals, and voting mechanisms are in place to ensure that the direction of the SUI blockchain aligns with the interests of its users. This level of engagement is particularly appealing to retail investors who value transparency and active participation in the projects they support.

Security remains a top priority for the SUI blockchain, with ongoing efforts to implement best practices and robust protocols. The platform utilizes cutting-edge cryptographic techniques to safeguard user assets and maintain the integrity of the network. Regular security audits and community-driven initiatives help identify vulnerabilities, ensuring that the ecosystem remains resilient against potential threats. For investors and developers alike, the commitment to security enhances confidence in the platform, making it an attractive choice for building and investing in blockchain solutions.

Looking ahead, the roadmap for the SUI blockchain is ambitious and filled with potential. Future developments are expected to focus on expanding the ecosystem through enhanced interoperability with other blockchains, introducing new features, and fostering a broader array of use cases across various industries. As the SUI community continues to grow, the platform is poised to become a significant player in the blockchain space, attracting attention from both seasoned investors and newcomers eager to explore the opportunities that SUI presents. With its strong foundation and forward-thinking approach, SUI is well-positioned for sustained growth and innovation in the ever-evolving cryptocurrency landscape.

Upcoming Features and Enhancements

The SUI ecosystem is on the verge of significant advancements, with various upcoming features and enhancements poised to elevate its functionality and appeal. One notable enhancement is the introduction of more robust smart contract capabilities. These improvements will allow developers to create more complex and efficient decentralized applications (dApps) that can cater to diverse industries. By enabling advanced features such as multi-signature wallets and automated execution conditions, the SUI platform aims to attract a larger pool of developers and projects, fostering innovation and increasing user engagement.

In addition to smart contract enhancements, SUI is set to roll out improved governance mechanisms that will empower the community. These mechanisms will enable token holders to participate more actively in decision-making processes, ensuring that the direction of the SUI ecosystem aligns with the interests of its users. This shift towards a more inclusive governance structure is essential in building trust and transparency, particularly for retail investors who seek assurance that their voices will be heard in the development of the platform. Enhanced voting protocols and proposal management systems will facilitate more efficient community engagement.

Security remains a paramount concern in the cryptocurrency space, and SUI is committed to bolstering its security protocols. Upcoming features will include advanced encryption techniques and automated auditing systems designed to identify vulnerabilities before they can be exploited. These enhancements will not only protect users' assets but also elevate the overall integrity of the SUI blockchain. As security remains a top priority for meme coin enthusiasts and serious investors alike, these measures will help instill confidence in the SUI ecosystem and its future prospects.

Moreover, the SUI roadmap outlines plans for expanding its use cases across various industries. With integrations into sectors such as finance, supply chain, and gaming, SUI aims to demonstrate the versatility of its blockchain technology. Upcoming partnerships with established companies will further validate the utility of SUI's solutions. As these initiatives unfold, they will showcase the potential for SUI to disrupt traditional business models and provide new opportunities for retail investors looking for innovative projects in the cryptocurrency landscape.

Finally, the SUI team is actively working on enhancing user experience through intuitive interfaces and streamlined onboarding processes. Recognizing that entry barriers can deter potential users, SUI is focusing on making its platform as accessible as possible. Features like simplified wallet management, educational resources, and responsive customer support will ensure that both newcomers and seasoned investors can navigate the ecosystem with ease. As SUI continues to evolve, these enhancements will play a crucial role in attracting a diverse audience and solidifying its position as a leader in the blockchain space.

Long-Term Vision for SUI

The long-term vision for SUI is centered around establishing a robust and scalable blockchain ecosystem that meets the diverse needs of its users while fostering innovation and collaboration. As the cryptocurrency landscape continues to evolve, SUI aims to position itself as a leader in delivering high-performance solutions that cater to developers, enterprises, and individual users alike. This vision encompasses not only the technical aspects of the SUI blockchain but also its role in shaping the future of decentralized applications (dApps) and smart contracts, making it a pivotal player within the broader cryptocurrency market.

One of the key components of SUI's long-term vision is the commitment to enhancing the user experience through seamless integration and intuitive interfaces. This focus on usability will encourage wider adoption among retail investors and everyday users, who may be intimidated by complex blockchain technology. By simplifying interactions with the SUI ecosystem, the platform aims to attract a diverse demographic, including those who may have previously been hesitant to engage with cryptocurrencies. This strategy aligns with the goal of making blockchain accessible to everyone, thereby expanding the user base and fostering community growth.

Another critical aspect of SUI's roadmap involves the continuous development of its smart contract capabilities. By prioritizing flexibility and security, SUI seeks to empower developers to create innovative dApps that address real-world problems across various industries. The long-term vision includes fostering partnerships with businesses and organizations that can leverage SUI's technology for their own applications. As more use cases emerge, SUI will establish itself as a go-to platform for developers looking to build scalable and efficient solutions, further solidifying its presence in the competitive blockchain landscape.

SUI's governance model is also integral to its long-term vision, emphasizing community involvement and transparent decision-making processes. By actively engaging its user base in governance, SUI not only builds trust but also ensures that the platform evolves in a manner that reflects the needs and desires of its community. This participatory approach will empower token holders to contribute to the direction of the ecosystem, creating a sense of ownership and encouraging sustained investment and interest in SUI.

Finally, the security protocols and best practices that underpin SUI's architecture are designed to instill confidence among users, especially retail investors who may be wary of potential risks in the cryptocurrency space. The vision includes rigorous audits, ongoing assessments of security measures, and a commitment to staying ahead of emerging threats. By prioritizing security, SUI aims to create an environment where users can transact and interact with peace of mind, ultimately supporting the long-term growth and sustainability of the ecosystem. Through these multifaceted initiatives, SUI is poised to make a significant impact on the future of blockchain technology and its applications.

Challenges and Opportunities Ahead

The landscape of cryptocurrencies is constantly evolving, presenting both challenges and opportunities for investors and enthusiasts alike. As we delve into the SUI ecosystem, it becomes evident that while the technology holds immense potential, several hurdles must be navigated to fully realize its capabilities. Issues such as regulatory uncertainty, scalability concerns, and competition from established blockchain platforms pose significant challenges. Investors must stay informed and agile, as the dynamic nature of the market can lead to rapid shifts in sentiment and opportunity.

One of the key opportunities within the SUI ecosystem lies in its innovative approach to smart contracts and decentralized applications (dApps). The SUI blockchain is designed with performance and flexibility in mind, enabling developers to create dApps that can seamlessly integrate with various industries. This adaptability opens the door for retail investors to engage with new projects and technologies that could yield substantial returns. The ability to participate in early-stage projects through token sales or governance mechanisms can provide unique investment opportunities that are often not available in traditional markets.

Community involvement and governance are also pivotal in shaping the future of the SUI ecosystem. As more users and developers contribute to its growth, the decentralized nature of the platform fosters an environment where collective decision-making can thrive. This presents a unique opportunity for investors to not only benefit from potential financial gains but also play a role in the evolution of the technology. Engaging with the community, whether through forums, social media, or direct participation in governance, allows investors to stay at the forefront of developments and influence the trajectory of the SUI ecosystem.

Security remains a critical concern in the world of cryptocurrencies, and the SUI platform is no exception. As the ecosystem grows, so too does the risk of vulnerabilities and attacks. However, with challenges come opportunities for innovation in security protocols. Developers are continuously working on enhancing the platform's security measures, ensuring that user assets and data are safeguarded. For retail investors, understanding these protocols and the measures in place can provide confidence in the technology's resilience, making it a more attractive option for investment.

Looking ahead, the roadmap for SUI outlines several exciting developments that could further transform its landscape. With advancements in scalability solutions, user experience enhancements, and new use cases emerging across various industries, the potential for growth is significant. Investors and enthusiasts should keep a close eye on these developments, as they not only represent potential financial opportunities but also the ongoing evolution of blockchain technology as a whole. As the SUI ecosystem continues to expand, those who remain informed and engaged will be best positioned to capitalize on the opportunities that lie ahead.

www.ingramcontent.com/pod-product-compliance
Lightning Source LLC
Chambersburg PA
CBHW030052230526
45471CB00003B/1067